PIANO • VOCAL • GUITAR

TOP CHRISTIAN HITS '09–'10

ISBN 978-1-4234-9084-5

HAL•LEONARD®
CORPORATION

7777 W. BLUEMOUND RD. P.O. BOX 13819 MILWAUKEE, WI 53213

Visit Hal Leonard Online at
www.halleonard.com

ALIVE AGAIN

Words and Music by MATT MAHER
and JASON INGRAM

Moderate Rock beat

I woke up in dark- / -ness, sur-round-ed by si - lence.__ Oh, where,__ where have __ I gone?__

BORN AGAIN

Words by MAC POWELL
Music by THIRD DAY

Well, to-day I ___ found my-

self, ___ af - ter search - ing all these ___ years. And the

CLOSER TO LOVE

Words and Music by MATHEW KEARNEY,
JOSIAH BELL and ROBERT MARVIN

Moderately

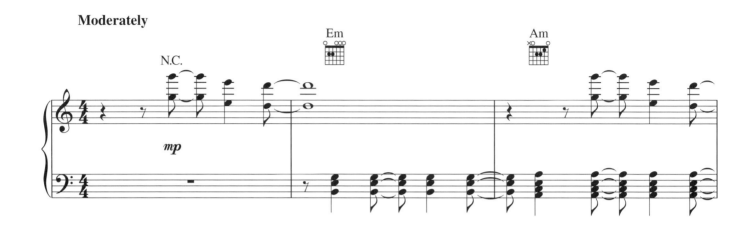

She got the call to-day, one out ___ of the gray.

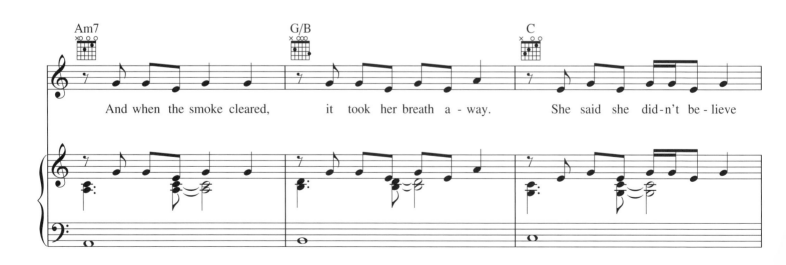

And when the smoke cleared, it took her breath a - way. She said she did-n't be - lieve

Pull me clos - er to love. _____

CITY ON OUR KNEES

Words and Music by TOBY McKEEHAN,
JAMES MOORE and CARY BARLOWE

To Coda

GLORY TO GOD FOREVER

Words and Music by STEVE FEE
and VICKY BEECHING

Be - fore the world was __ made,
Cre - at - or God, You __ gave

be - fore You spoke it to be,
me breath so I _____ could praise

You were the King of ____ kings,
Your great and match - less ___ name

yeah, You were, yeah, You were.
all my days, all my days.

And now You're reign - ing ___ still,
So let my whole life ___ be

Recorded a half step lower.

HEAVEN IS THE FACE

Words and Music by
STEVEN CURTIS CHAPMAN

Heav-en is the face of a lit-tle girl ___ with
heav-en is the sound of her breath-ing deep, ___

dark brown eyes that dis-ap-pear ___ when she smiles.
ly-ing on my chest, fall-ing fast a-sleep ___ while I sing.

And heav-en is the place where she calls my name, ___ says,
And heav-en is the weight of her in my arms, ___ be -

GOD YOU REIGN

Words and Music by LINCOLN BREWSTER
and MIA FIELDES

You paint _ the night, _
You part _ the seas, _

You count _ the stars _ and You call them by name. _
You move _ the moun - tains with the words that You say.

HOLD MY HEART

Words and Music by JASON INGRAM,
PHILLIP LaRUE and MIKE DONEHEY

How long must I pray, _

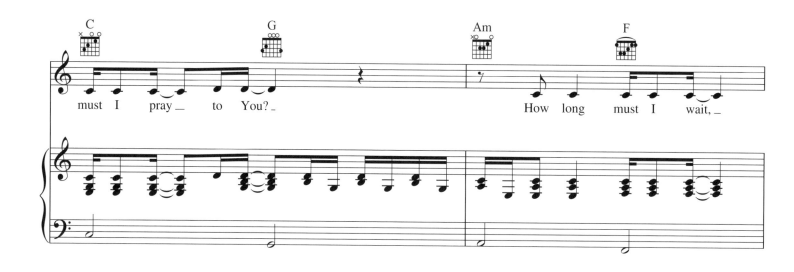

must I pray _ to You? _

How long must I wait, _

must I wait _ for You? _

How long till I see Your face, _

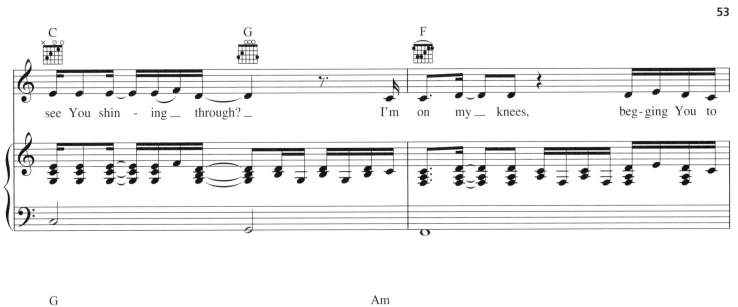

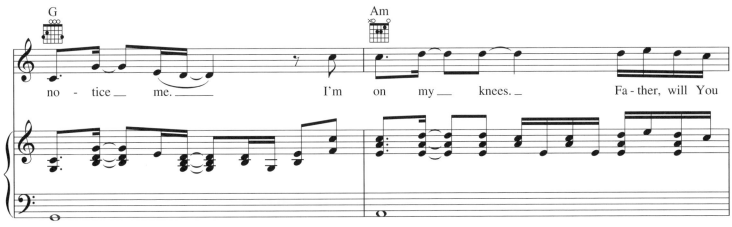

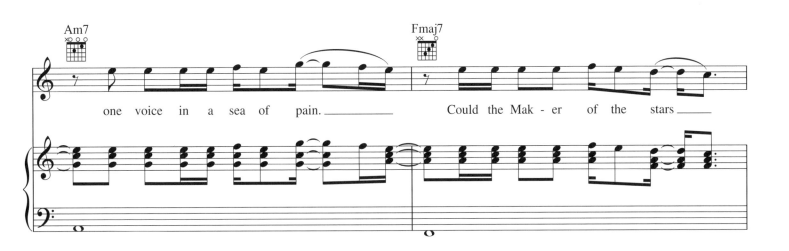

HOPE NOW

Words and Music by
RYAN GREGG

HOW HE LOVES

Words and Music by
JOHN MARK McMILLAN

how He ___ loves us. ___ Oh, oh, how He ___

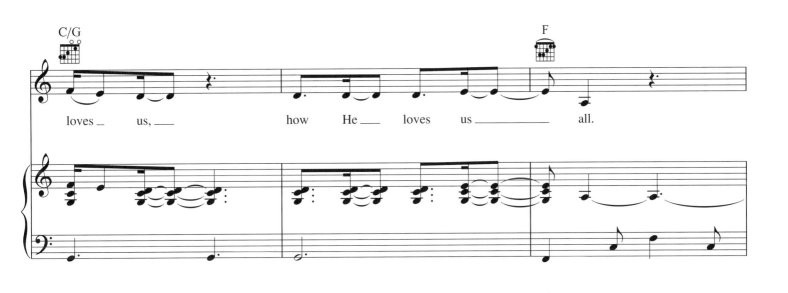

loves ___ us, ___ how He ___ loves us ___ all.

I WILL RISE

Words and Music by CHRIS TOMLIN,
JESSE REEVES, LOUIE GIGLIO
and MATT MAHER

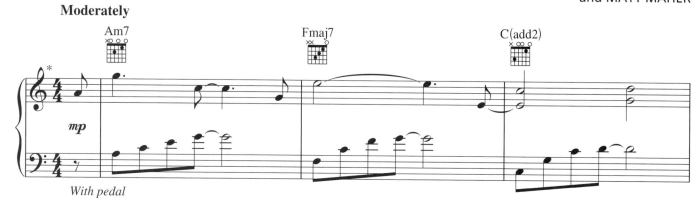

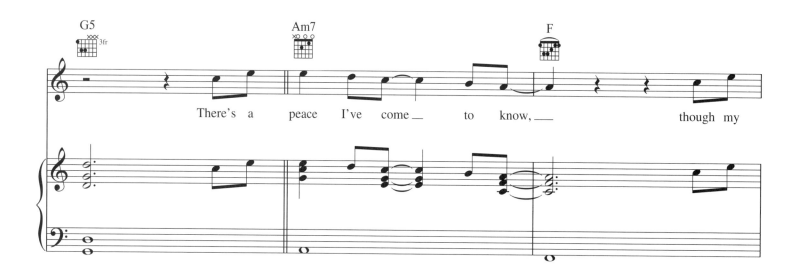

There's a peace I've come to know, though my

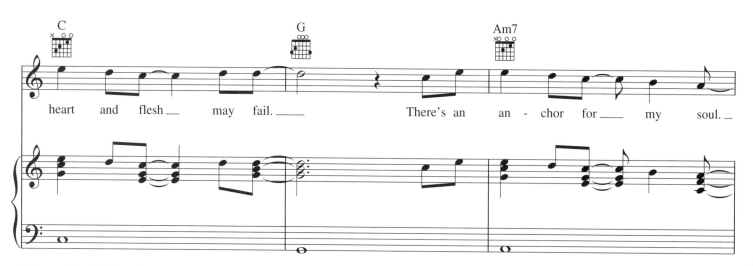

heart and flesh may fail. There's an an-chor for my soul.

* Recorded a half step lower.

LEAD ME TO THE CROSS

Words and Music by
BROOKE FRASER

Recorded a half step lower.

THE LOST GET FOUND

Words and Music by BEN GLOVER
and BRITT NICOLE

Recorded a half step lower.

THE MOTIONS

Words and Music by SAM MIZELL,
MATTHEW WEST and JASON HOUSER

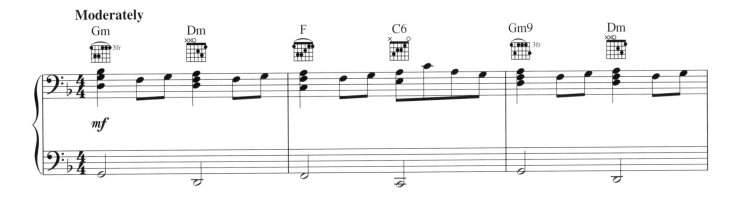

This might hurt, ___ it's not safe, ___
No re - grets, ___ not this time. ___

___ but I know that I've got - ta make ___ a change. I don't care ___ if I break; ___
___ I'm gon - na let my ___ heart de - feat ___ my mind, let Your love ___ make me whole. ___

I don't wan-na go, I don't wan-na go _____ through the mo -

- tions. (Take me all the way.) ___

I don't wan-na go through the mo - tions. ___

MORE BEAUTIFUL YOU

Words and Music by JONNY DIAZ
and KATE YORK

To Coda

to fill __ a pur-pose that on-ly you __ could do, __ so there could nev-er

be __ a more beau-ti-ful __ you.

Lit-tle girl, twen-ty-one, the things that you've al-read-y done; an-y-thing to get a-head. __ And you

SPEAKING LOUDER THAN BEFORE

Words and Music by
JEREMY CAMP

Recorded a half step lower.

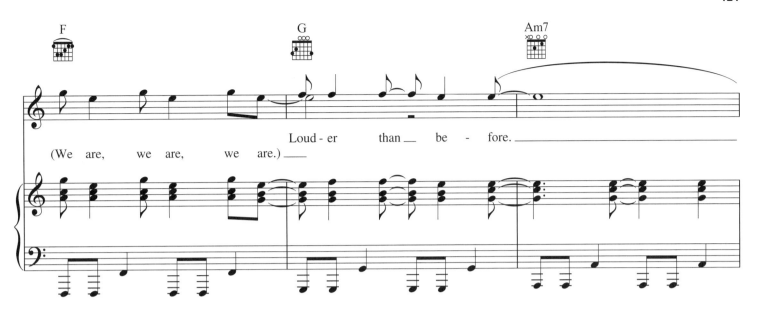

Loud - er than ___ be - fore. _____

(We are, we are, we are.) ____

We are speak - ing loud - er than ___ be - fore, __

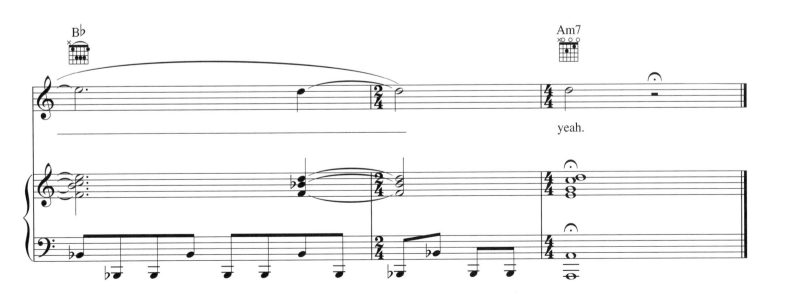

yeah.

UNTIL THE WHOLE WORLD HEARS

Words and Music by MARK HALL,
ROGER GLIDEWELL, JASON McARTHUR
and BERNIE HERMS

Lord, I want to feel with Your heart____ and see the world thru Your eyes.____

* *Recorded a half step lower.*

WHAT FAITH CAN DO

Words and Music by SCOTT DAVIS
and SCOTT KRIPPAYNE

Ev - 'ry - bod - y falls some - times. ___ Got - ta find the strength to rise ___ ___ from the ash - es and make a new ___ be - gin - ning. An - y - one can feel the ache. ___ You think it's more than you can take, ___

132

It does-n't mat-ter what you've heard; ___ "im-pos-si-ble" is not a word. ___

___ It's just a rea-son for some-one not ___ to try. ___

Ev-'ry-bod-y's scared to death ___ when they de-cide to take that step ___

___ out on the wa-ter. but it-'ll be ___ al-right. ___

YOU'RE NOT SHAKEN

Words and Music by PHIL STACEY,
JASON INGRAM, MATT BRONLEEWE
and ANDRE FROMM

Moderately slow, in 2

I am sink - ing in a riv - er that is rag -
- bling in the dark - ness of my own

- ing.
____ fear.
I am drown - ing; will I ev -
All the ques - tions with no an -

- er rise ____ to breathe ____ a - gain? ____ I wan - na know
- swers so grip ____ me while ____ I'm here. ____ And I may nev - er know

* Recorded a half step lower.

140